Pulling the Invisible but Heavy Cart

Last Poems

Pulling the Invisible but Heavy Cart

Last Poems

PETER EVERWINE

Edited by

Bill Broder, C.G. Hanzlicek, Christopher Buckley

Afterword by

David St. John

STEPHEN F. AUSTIN STATE UNIVERSITY PRESS

For information about permission to reproduce selections from this book, contact *Permissions*, at sfapress@sfasu.edu

For information about special discounts for bulk purchases, contact *Distribution* at sfapress@sfasu.edu or 1-936-468-1078

Production manager: Kimberly Verhines

ISBN 978-1-62288-543-5

Stephen F. Austin State University Press
P.O. Box 13007 SFA Station
Nacogdoches, Texas 75962
sfapress@sfasu.edu
www.sfasu.edu/sfapress
936-468-1078

CONTENTS

Acknowledgments ⌣· 11

Introduction C.G. Hanzlicek ⌣· 13

New Poems

I

The Kiskiminetas River ⌣· 17

Lines Written for Elmo Castelnuovo ⌣· 19

Saint Joseph of the Mines ⌣· 21

156 Main Street ⌣· 22

A Small Story ⌣· 23

"Haunted Heart" ⌣· 24

We Were Running ⌣· 25

The Day ⌣· 26

II

Making Salamis ⌣· 29

For Ava, in the Coming Days ⌣· 30

A Credo for Fallen Arches ⌣· 31

Names 1-7 ⌣· 32

Joe's Garden ⌣· 39

From the Kitchen Window ⌣· 40

Blackbird ⌣· 41

Nellie ⌣· 42

Big John and the Banjo ⌣· 43

III

Needs ⤙ 47

Stella ⤙ 48

The Garage ⤙ 49

Elegy for a Gray Wolf ⤙ 51

Two Doves ⤙ 52

Old Women ⤙ 53

The Depot ⤙ 54

I Thought ⤙ 55

Still Life ⤙ 56

At the Hermitage ⤙ 57

Doppler Scan: Deep Vein Thrombosis ⤙ 59

How it is (Later) ⤙ 60

Notes ⤙ 61

Supplement: Prose Selections, Comments, and Interviews

Introduction by Bill Broder ⤙ 65

II. "Concerning 'In the Last Days' " ⤙ 67

III. "Feeling Back to That Voice" an interview by Jon Veinberg &
        Christopher Buckley, 1983 ⤙ 69

IV. from an interview by Chard deNiord, edited by Bill Broder ⤙ 90

V. "In the Moment" an interview by Jon Veinberg &
        Christopher Buckley, 2016 ⤙ 84

VI. from a *Kenyon Review* Conversation with Claire Oleson, 2018 ⤙ 103

Afterword, David St. John ⤙ 107

As if words were like old men
I knew as a boy, walking slowly homeward
at dusk, bent, their hands clasped
behind their backs, pulling an invisible
but heavy cart.

Peter Everwine

For Connie Barbara

&

for my family—those gone, lost, present, to come—
each and every one of you

Acknowledgments:

The author wishes to thank the editors of the following publications, in which these new poems were first published:

A Small Clearing, copyright 2016 by Peter Everwine, published by Aureole Press in a limited edition chapbook.

We Were Running, a limited edition letterpress broadside by Greenhouse Review Press, 2018.

American Journal of Poetry	"Making Salamis"
Askew	"Depot"
Aureole Press	"From the Kitchen Window"
Five Points	"The Hermitage"
Great River Review	"Saint Joseph of the Mines"
HUBBUB	"156 Main Street"
	"Haunted Heart"
	"We Were Running"
The Kenyon Review	"Needs"
	"How it is (Later,)"
	"I Thought"
Miramar	"Blackbird"
	"Depot"
	"Still Life"
	"Stella"
New Letters	"Lines Written for Elmo Castelnuovo"
	"Nellie"
	"A Credo for Fallen Arches," and
	"One Day"
The Southern Review	"The Kiskiminetas River"

"The Kiskiminetas River" was reprinted in *The Best American Poetry* 2016, edited by Edward Hirsch and David Lehman (New York: Scribner's, 2016.)

"A Small Story" and "One Day" appeared in the Poetry Foundation's *American Life in Poetry.* I want to thank Ted Kooser and Pat Emile of the University of Nebraska.

"Concerning 'In the Last Days'" by Peter Everwine originally appeared in "Origins: Poets on the Composition Process," *Poetry East* #55 (2005) edited by Richard Jones.

"At the Hermitage" is anthologized in *Universal Oneness: An Anthology of Magnum Opus Poems from around the World* by Authorspress, New Delhi, India.

"We Were Running" received the Kenneth O. Hanson Prize, my thanks to *HUBBUB*.

I am indebted to friends who have given me support and the benefits of their criticism, especially Bill Broder, Chris Buckley, C G. Hanzlicek, Connie Lake, Robert Mezey, and my late friend and colleague, Philip Levine, who I deeply miss. My thanks to all.

Feeling Back To That Voice—An Interview with Peter Everwine, by Jon Veinberg & Christopher Buckley, 1983.   *Snake Nation Review*

Some remarks by Peter Everwine about his craft gleaned from an interview by Chard deNiord, in Grafton, Vermont on July 18, 2010., 48/2 Fall 2018.   the *Iowa Review*

In the Moment: An Interview with Peter Everwine by Christopher Buckley and Jon Veinberg 2016.   *New Letters, Vol. 83* No. 1

Peter Everwine: A Kenyon Review Conversation (Short Interview with Claire Oleson) Aug. 2018.   *Kenyon Review*

Peter Everwine

Peter Everwine and I were friends for 52 years. He called me his poetry brother, but truth be told, that was pure flattery. Our relationship was more like mentor and mentee, but to me he was even more than a mentor: he was a lodestar, my guide to navigating the currents of both life and poetry.

Peter was, above all, a man of enormous kindness. He radiated a warmth that everyone around him felt. After people, his great love was poetry, and he cherished every poet from the Aztecs to Christopher Smart to the great moderns of Middle Europe and Israel. After poetry came music, especially 50's and 60's jazz; his favorite jazz musician was the tenor saxophone player, Ben Webster. And then there was string band music. In his day, he was quite adept at the banjo and sat in with many musicians in the rural beer joints of Fresno County. Late career, he played with a group called the String Bandits, and he was fond of saying that the group got its name because when anyone paid them to play, it was highway robbery. To the list of his loves has to be added art, both primitive and modern, which he collected avidly.

Reading through his last poems, I am struck again by their beauty. They speak in a singular voice, one of clarity and simple diction, and always the voice responds to passion, not poetic fashion. It seems a little quaint to speak of beauty in poetry, but in these poems, forged in a lovely quietude, there is no roaring, no clamor, just words that arise from the surrounding silence, words that strike one as infallibly well-spoken. His poems have an inner glow, like moonlight on dew. They speak to us of the things that matter: family, love, the grace of the physical world, and our sorrow that we must someday part from these things. I love the poems because they belong utterly to him. I love them because they embrace the world. I love them because they elevate my species.

Many of the old Navajo songs have the refrain, "I walk in beauty." In the very words you can see the singer walking atop the mesas or through the canyons of their homeland, feeling the power of the landscape flood the body.

Peter, old friend, you walk in beauty.

—C. G. Hanzlicek

I

The Kiskiminetas River

It begins in the seepage of salt wells,
as if waking from a dream of the sea
before it gathers itself and runs

for twenty-seven restless, hard-working
miles, only to lose itself, swept inland
toward Pittsburgh and the vast Ohio Valley.

Kiskiminetas: the Lenape name means
clear stream of many bends or break camp,
the etymology unclear but apt:

wherever the Lenape tried to settle,
someone came along and moved them
to a place no one wanted.

My grandfather, in Italy a farmer, dug coal
not far from where it empties into the Allegheny.
His sons would inherit and divide his labor:

coal mines, steel mills, foundries.
The river turned sulfur-orange and stank
from all the mines draining into it—

another putrid seam of the earth.
Even the rocks of the riverbed took on
the petrified figures of the lost:

Shy Charlie, who took a header off the bridge;
Bobby, who slipped into the current
like a sack of sewage; my father, who flew

his car over its cindered embankment
in the hard winter of my birth.
Nothing is held in place by a name;

but the river changes and is changeless.
The mines are now closed; the small towns
seem emptier and forlorn at night;

the river runs clear, its surface
shifting in the glint of morning light
or the passing shadows of its seasons.

On the bluffs, overlooking the valley,
my grandfather and his sons have come to rest
among the now, or soon to be, forgotten.

Lines Written for Elmo Castelnuovo

It's not time that passes, it's you, it's I
    —Rutger Kopland

In winter, by late afternoon, it's almost dark
when you come home from the mine. I hear
the front gate creak and the metallic clink
of your pail before you round the corner
by the back steps where I've been waiting.
In the sharp chill of the air, the mineral
undercurrent of damp earth and shale
comes with you. You turn down the collar
of your shirt and let water from the pump
pour down your face and nape, the skin above
your undershirt pale as the crescent moon visible
above the darker mass of the hills.

                *   *   *

You drive for hours, heading nowhere; you walk
the streets at night and argue with the moon—
something hidden and manic in you emerged,
almost unnoticed, until at last you huddled
homeless and bewildered under a pile
of coats in an alleyway no wider
than the mines you entered as a young man.
The rat scuttling in the garbage bin, the cat
stalking the rat, did they become your familiars?
And the passersby, who glanced at you and hurried
on their way, did they believe you were invisible?
Did the tag knotted to your toe say nameless?

                *   *   *

What I loved was the touch of your calloused hand
on my head, the coal-rimmed hollows of your eyes.
If you returned now from the sooty underworld
in which you dwell, you would not recognize me.
The gate is gone; the house and those who lived in it
are hidden elsewhere. Only the crescent moon
and darkling hills are as you left them. Come back
as you were, if only for a moment. I'm waiting
by the back steps. The kitchen window casts
its light; at the laden table the absent prepare
for your arrival. You will be hungry and tired,
as in those years through which our lives passed.

Saint Joseph of the Mines

Pine Run, a small coal-mining camp,
is gone, its shanties rotted and fallen-in,
abandoned to wild grapevines, the interlace
of bramble and woods, as if it never was.

My mother was born there, but in later years
not even she could find it. She remembered,
as a child, falling headlong into cinders
by the railroad spur and gashing her knee;

she stopped crying, she said, because she saw,
next to her hand, a tiny coal-black statue
of Saint Joseph, which she brought home
and held while her wound was bandaged.

It stood on her dresser all her life, a sign,
she believed, given to her for mercy's sake.
Mercy was hard to come by in the mines,
and the gift, a covenant for hard times.

After my mother's death, I buried her
in the shale hills not far from where she was born.
There is in graveyards an immense loneliness.
I don't believe in the communion of saints,

I don't believe in the promise that the consolation
for our pain dwells in the mansions of the Lord,
but I buried Saint Joseph of the Mines with her:
in my unbelief, bless her belief.

156 Main Street

The house is empty, but the rooms keep hidden
what we left behind: the crumpled sock
in the closet, odd buttons, pins, a feather from
a lady's Sunday hat, a child's lead soldier.

If walls could only talk! But they do,
though only in an ancient alphabet
we tried to learn—that sibilance under the eaves
at night, that rub and click of consonants,

as if they repeated and repeated the rumor
that a day is coming when the house
will disappear into its own emptiness.
That day, dear house of my youth, has come.

And so the wind moves
through the cherry tree, clouds pass
on their way to the sea, the journey
of the stars is nightly made visible.

In the vacant lot, a common thrush
picks his way through a maze of rubble,
searching for something to fill himself
before he sings.

A Small Story

When Mrs. McCausland comes to mind
she slips through a gap in oblivion
and walks down her front steps, in her hand
a small red velvet pillow she tucks
under the head of Old Jim Schreiber,
who is lying dead-drunk against the curb
of busy Market Street. Then she turns,
labors up the steps and is gone. . .

A small story. Or rather, the memory
of a story I heard as a boy. The witnesses
are not to be found, the steps lead nowhere,
the pillow has collapsed into a thread of dust. . .
Do the dead come back only to remind us
they, too, were once among the living,
and that the story we make of our lives
is a mystery of luminous, but uncertain moments,
a shuffle of images we carry toward sleep—
Mrs. McCausland with her velvet pillow,
Old Jim at peace—a story like a small
clearing in the woods at night, seen
from the windows of a passing train.

"Haunted Heart"

Charlie Haden (1937-2014)

A late evening in July. I'm slow-dancing
alone to "Haunted Heart" as Haden's bass
blossoms and fades in the room like a passing
resonance of time. "The nostalgia of
beautiful moments," he said, meaning the ache
and yearning of song, moments like scenes
dissolving in a film to which one could return.
He understood how haunted a heart can be,
though the body sways to its own sweet music.
I dance a step back, dance a step back,
in a room that suddenly is crowded.

We Were Running

in memory of Annie

We were running up the slope of a hill
that dog and I, an early winter rain
beginning to fall, wind-driven and sharp,
the clouds so black the edges of the hills
were etched and incandescent. That dog
and I were running, the two of us
apart and yet together, and even now,
in the solitude of a quiet hour—the days
and that dog long gone—I can follow
those far-blown traces of unexpected joy
and find my way back again: heart wild,
lungs filling with the breath of winter,
and that dog beside me running headlong
into the world without end.

The Day

We walked at the edge of the sea, the dog
still young then, running ahead of us.

Few people. Gulls. A flock of pelicans
circled beyond the swells, then closed
their wings and dropped head-long
into the dazzle of light and sea. You clapped
your hands, the day grew brilliant.

Later we sat at a small table
with wine and food that tasted of the sea.

A perfect day, we said to one another,
so that even when the day ended
and the lights of houses among the hills
came on like a scattering of embers,
we watched it leave without regret.

And that night, easing myself toward sleep,
I thought how blindly we stumble ahead
with such hope, a light flares briefly—Ah, Happiness!
then we turn and go on our way again.

But happiness, too, goes on its way,
and years from where we were, I lie awake
in the dark and suddenly it returns—
that day by the sea, that happiness,

though it is not the same happiness,
not the same darkness.

II

Making Salamis

It was a game. We called it "Making Salamis."
To make them, you rubbed the index finger up
and down the ridges along your nose or across
your neck until you rolled some cylinders
of grease and dirt that resembled miniature turds,
inedible to any form of life but flies.
We were ignorant boys, socially inept,
suspicious of the world and the admonition
of our elders to "make something of yourself"—
we, who knew almost nothing about ourselves
except that we were good at making salamis.
Which may explain to you why the simple act
of making them brought to our anxious lives
such gross, barbaric and hilarious delight.

For Ava, in the Coming Days

Your first glimpse of me frightened you
and made you cry: a stranger, scraggly beard
and glasses, a slack and weather-beaten face.
I can't blame you. Even I, at times,
startle, catching myself in the bad light
of a bathroom mirror. So recently arrived,
you like one foot in the circle of the familiar.

I watch you at dinner—mushing your food as if
you knew the truth of living hand to mouth,
slinging the heft and sweet muck of it
with such delight it turns your tears to laughter.
I might wish for you the gift already yours:
May you hold this joy in mind and turn to it
when you have grown, dear child, decorous and civil.

A Credo For Fallen Arches

Because as a child I saw the luminous green aureole
of my feet at Kaufman's shoe department in Pittsburgh,
I believe in the inner sanctum of the body.

Because my parents insisted on buying me hard
leather inserts to repair my broken arches,
I believe obligation wears a hidden sword.

Because for years I walked on a road of stones
and could not run with a boy's abandon,
I believe the bird was the first creation in paradise.

Because I walked on the sides of my feet
when I left the waters of my exile,
I believe in the footprints of the invisible.

Because a woman took my feet in her hands
and did not find them ugly and unfit,
I believe caritas is the Balm of Gilead.

Because though I press heavily upon the earth
and anchor myself to it, as best I can,
I believe it, too, is a mote of dust, a glint of starlight.

Because I am old and love the earth, no longer knowing
the difference between gravity and gravitas,
I believe in the unreasonable faith and fidelity of my feet.

    Laudate!

NAMES

1

My prodigal grandfather, after many years, has returned from Italy. I am a boy and have never met the man who enters the room, stooped with age and his early labor in the mines. He has brought me a gift: a handful of tiny, brightly colored paper parasols. Only many years from now will I identify them as ornaments for exotic, tropical drinks. Perhaps I am inventing this—no, not our meeting but the gift— both are mysterious, giving off an aura of a world I do not know. He gazes at me with his faded, old man's eyes and cups my face in his hand. As if we had met somewhere before I entered the world, he calls me by my secret name: *Junio,* he says. *Eh, come sta, Junio?*

2

I wanted to name my first-born "Elmo" but my wife wouldn't have it. I told her about Elmo Tanner, the whistling virtuoso. I explained St. Elmo's fire, how his electrical and eerie energy was perfectly suited to the age in which we lived. She wasn't moved. So we named him after a saint, of course, and it all turned out well. There are many names for love, and I love him, saint or no. I gave him an Italian middle name that few know or ever use. I sometimes wonder if he dreams at night of dancing a Tarantella in Naples, the men clapping, women flashing their eyes at him as he whirls around the piazza in his beautifully-made shoes.

3

I wanted to name my second-born "Dominic," after a balding, Dago trumpet player, a sessions man who played scales for hours to strengthen his embouchure. He was eccentric and practiced only after rubbing warm olive oil on his head and wrapping it in a turban of hot towels. My wife called me crazy and named him David, after one of her family. I was writing poetry at the time so I slipped it in as a middle name. It made a trochee followed by a dactyl. If you lagged a little behind the beat, and phrased it right, man, it was beautiful! My son developed a flair for sweetness, a big heart and a bald spot.

4

Merle was my stepfather's name. His people were country folks: apple orchards, cows, pigsties. He went to college, came back from WWI as a small town doctor. In America, you can re-invent yourself. He added the letter J before his name, a hook on which to hang a new identity. "Mornin' J M," said the local banker. "Afternoon, J M," said the druggist, from whom he bought his cigars. He ordered a Buick; drove it to the annual county fairs. He liked being around the sweet snuffling of animals, the baked pies in the Home Pavilion.

5

I had a young beagle I named "Watson," thinking he would grow into a hound worthy of Sherlock Holmes' famed associate. I, of course, imagined myself as Sherlock; together we would track down the wariest rabbits in the woods. On our first hunt Watson got lost, tangled himself in wild grape vines, and howled in loneliness until I found and rescued him. Poor Watson! Shortly after this, he developed a disease that drove him through the house, butting blindly into baseboards, table legs, as if desperate to breathe the wild perfume of rabbit through a nose meant for greatness.

6

Cousin Benny liked to sit in a miner's crouch, leaning his back against the garage door and looking at the view from his alley. He could see where the hill fell off into the seam between valleys. He thought of the creek down there, Buttermilk Falls, near the old mine shaft and the bramble patches where he loved to hunt rabbits. Benny was a misogynist who loudly and often publically referred to his wife as "a horse's ass." It got so bad people began to think it was her natural name. In revenge, she furnished the house in faux-French, with Cupids clamping onto the lamps. Which is why Benny liked sitting in the alley, thinking about murdering rabbits and the simple days of Buttermilk Falls.

7

She has one of those double first names that Appalachian folks often give to girls: Connie Barbara. Either one name is not good enough, or two make up for being born a girl. No matter, I like the sound of hers. In our years together, I've called her by a lot of names—some loving, some private, some harmful and bitter. Being close to someone for a time is like a series of accidents where people gather to talk about what's happening. I will say this: some nights, when I watched her sleep, you might not believe how beautiful her name was when it rose to my lips.

Joe's Garden

for Joe Millar

Joe has a garden on his desk growing
in the best light a window can provide.

He's planted it in fountain pens, and no,
I'm not inventing this: he calls it "The Garden"—

a double row of hollow wooden tubes
like tiny fence posts bored in odd diameters.

From each tube, Joe plucks, like a flower, the pen
that fits his need: black for the sullen days,

deep blue when happiness looms, the marbled colors
for confusion when the anxious hours arrive.

Lucky the poet for whom organic form
blooms close at hand, and yet how difficult

it is, these days, finding a pen to fit
the darkening fields that lie beyond the window.

From the Kitchen Window

in memory of Alice Zacharias

Oh, hain't it grand! she said, mornings
long ago, looking out her kitchen window—
the wooded hills and meadows opening
to the glory of first light, rose-colored finches
scuffing in the dirt, a random deer at field's edge.
But some days were born dark, and rivulets
of rain furrowed the yard. The sodden goats
huddled in their pen, wooded hills and meadows
were a child's scrawl. *Oh, hain't it grand!* she said,
as if gloom had no place in her heart.

It's something to love the world and know
it does not love you in return. For all her country ways,
she understood that woods and meadow,
bird and beast, were beyond the dominion
of her regard. And so the sorrow of her passing
was also the sorrow for a vanished world,
though even as I write these words, in memory
she turns to her kitchen window, *Oh,*
hain't it grand! she says, and yes, truly it is.

Blackbird

This morning a blackbird perches on the edge
of my imitation Roman fountain, leaps in,
fills the basin with himself, and thrashes
his wings with a sudden violence as the spout
of water spills over him; then jumps out,
shakes himself to a sheen, and twice again
he plunges, the water sloshing over the edge
as if he were a small, ferocious paddle-boat
beating upstream against a heavy current.

I know the usual explanations for his ritual:
bacteria, mites, a comb for stray feathers.
But you can't tell me a bird has no idea
of happiness, or that he doesn't seek delight
in the weight of water under his wings—
that rapture of substance, so unlike air,
holding him steady in its firm embrace—
as if you couldn't figure out happiness
if suddenly you leapt up from the chair
in which you sat and found yourself
flying above the pear tree in your yard.

Nellie

Philip Levine : 1928-2015

In your letters to me you signed yourself "Nellie",
the name you'd given to a cat you favored.
Touching, I thought; you, such fondness for a cat.
But I think you may have fooled me, friend, and named
the two of you after Nellie Fox, the White Sox
Hall of Famer, although the fox you meant
was a spirit animal—resilient, uncanny,
kindred to the seer and the seen, sly trickster, clown.
You had a painting of one in your study. As you worked,
it kept watch with you until you looked up
from the words you'd found, and time returned.
Animals, as you said, are passing from our lives,
and though it's of your quick spirit and passing I speak,
it seems fitting that I think of you now
as a fox high-tailing through a stubble field;
at your heels a pack of loud-mouth hounds
and hunters tricked out in their stylish uniforms,
you running just fast enough to let them think
they have a chance at you. Then, game-weary
of their brass announcements and theatrical airs, you slip
into the gathering shadows of the woods
laughing your ass off.

Big John and the Banjo

Big John had a stub finger on his left hand
and his ear leaned a little shy of pitch,
but he hammered his banjo, sitting gladsome
in the back corner of Dottie's Roadhouse Den
with Roy and Kenney as the dancers whirled by.

He once told me that as a younger man
he spent a season panning gold in a canyon
so snaky he took to wearing stovepipes to keep
from being bit, and the bright, percussive ping
of rattlers glancing off his galvanized legs
echoed from the canyon walls such shivery
and haunting sounds he couldn't forget them.
The canyon was a lonely place. That winter,
in a Lodi pawnshop, he bought a banjo
and taught himself the sounds he remembered.

A tall tale, of course. But the wonder of its making
was also its truth, and I thought of Sir John Davies,
who had imagined the universe as an orchestra—
one vast Elizabethan hum of its dancing parts;
and here is Big John, his country kin,
who was himself both instrument and witness
of the earth's improbable music, playing
in the orchestra of Dottie's Roadhouse Den,
his eyes half closed in bliss as the dancers
whirled by, whirled by, the dancers whirled by.

III

Needs

My mother planned for her funeral
as if it were a polar expedition,
and she paid cash in hand, that no one
could say of her that she was beholden.

Jobbed out for housework at the age of eleven,
she was schooled in serving the needs of others,
although it brought a stiffness to her heart
and a tongue that could hone words to an edge.

She lived alone, twice widowed, for fifty years,
cleaning one room a day, then starting over
until the day she reached up from her ladder
and found a shadow into which she fell.

And when it came time to leave forever
she wore the gown she chose, and her music,
"Over the Rainbow," played softly in the viewing room.
And there were flowers and wreathes—one bound

with a white ribbon bearing my name in gold,
which she herself had bought for the appointed hour
in case I forgot, and in plain view of others,
brought on both of us an unbearable shame.

Stella

(1915-1938)

Of all the stars in the sky that night,
what were the odds of being born
under the star of misfortune?

Twenty-three years. Bone thin,
pitted by acne, pulling hard for each breath
until your lungs caught fire.

You came to stay in "the sick room"
that was next to mine, kept it shuttered
against the day and dimly lit.

I was a frightened child; you were a cloud
of incense, a late night murmur of voices
behind the door, a tremor of weeping.

What measure of joy or wretchedness
was yours, I'll never know. But after your room
had emptied, I kept you hidden within me,

as if I remained the child I'd been, a stranger
more than kin, questions with no answer,
a dream of anxiety that troubled my days.

You died too young to know that every night
light falls on us from stars that were extinguished
a million years ago. Your brief life,

my longer one, what do they come to?
Pale star, blood of my blood, burnt ember of time,
how could we not belong to each other?

The Garage

Paolo Castelnuovo (1869-1942)

After a failed marriage, after I moved
into a small made-over garage off an alley,
I was afraid I'd spend my late years
like you, Grandfather, errant and alone.

Prodigal, after years in Piemonte, you lived in a shack
and each morning walked down from the brich
to the local Marconi Club for your cup of coffee—
black with a touch of grappa for the spirit's sake.

As a boy I met you only in a field of absence;
the others knew you as a millstone, heavy
as your hands had been—a bitterness they shared
as charity for the old man you'd become,

bent by time and the shallow mines you worked—
that is, when you chose to work. You had restless feet
when younger—a trouble you passed on to me.
I made you into an exotic and mysterious figure—

my grandfather, who could shatter a beer-mug
with his jaws and had sailed across the Atlantic
so often he knew the captains by their given names
as if they were constellations he steered by.

Old legends. Rumors. I moved you into my garage—
at night your shadow whispered in the tongue I knew
as a child and at first light, like a migrant bird,
you called me as in a dream. Your name was Paolo,

my middle name is Paul; our failures we held
in common. I don't know what I wanted from you—
a star to map the drifts of time and place?
a yearning hidden beneath the reach of words?

You left as you came. Grown old, Grandfather,
I spend my days still searching for words, my nights
with a touch of booze. I know so little of your life,
but for a while we lived together, making this poem.

Elegy for a Gray Wolf

The gray wolf, over the years,
had become demented, trotting
from one corner of his cage
to another without pause or rest.

I used to visit him on quiet
afternoons, drawn to his cage
yet appalled to bear witness
to his blind, unbearable rush.

I can't tell you if a wolf despairs,
or if an urgency of the spirit
can howl in silence until it stuns
the hammering heart into oblivion;

but he lived among passersby, an exhibit
and a curiosity. I speak here
of a gray wolf, bewildered and lost
in his own wilderness, who ran

as long and as far as he could before
he reached that place from which he started
and to which he had returned still heading
toward what he may have remembered.

Two Doves

Two doves have come to my fountain,
which is dry. Cocking their heads, they walk
around the rim, peering intently—this way,

that way—into the basin, as if bewildered
by the water's absence, its failure to appear
before the urgency of their thirst.

I have been negligent, and my feeling of guilt
is a long story. No one wants to hear it.
The beaver drowns in the trap. The wolf

howls its desolation. The exhausted yearling
falters in the snow that slowly covers it.
The gate to the garden closed behind us—

every beast of the field, the fowl of the air,
what could they do but follow us
into the world that opened before our eyes?

Old Women

I like old women in black shawls
who sit quietly against the wall of the house
late afternoons, warming themselves
in the sun, watching the hens strut

in the dirt yard, old women in the early mist
off the river who scrub their clothes
against stones that are as familiar
and worn as their own hands,

the old women, who smile at men
when being introduced, covering
their mouths like shy girls because
they have few teeth or none,

serious old women who have lived
in the same place all their lives
and lie down stiffly at night, hearing
a screech owl gossip from the chestnut tree

that someone was passing in the shadows
by the moonlit road, as if they had never heard
it call to them before, spreading the news
that they had always known.

The Depot

for Jon Veinberg

One by one they set their baggage on the platform
and, relieved of their burden, prepare to depart.

One holds a lucky coin in his hand.
One thinks of a pond he fished as a boy.

One whistles softly through pursed lips.
One keeps a sorrow in her heart.

One leaves behind the words that went unsaid.
One sees a window and runnels of winter rain.

Meanwhile the baggage has been stowed away
or lost in the confusion, because, as usual,

a crowd is milling about on the platform, waving
goodbye to those diminishing into distance.

I Thought

for Bill Broder

I thought I had traveled beyond the range
of the human eye or the ear's measure

but no, there was my house, standing
where it always stood, and the pot of red geraniums

I thought I would find something wondrous
and strange that I had never seen

but no, it was only the bird-lady rounding
the corner with her sack of stale loaves

I thought when I opened my door and called
"Is anyone home?" I heard

a voice I faintly recognized
or remembered from a dream I had

but no, it was only the old implacable
din of silence waiting for me to enter

and replenish its empty bowl

Still Life

That old man sitting on a garden bench
by the wind-ruffled pond, a stir of leaves
casting their shadows on a sun-lit afternoon…

Can you hear him? that murmur of syllables
like a hum falling into gaps of silence,
that slow breath of a sigh that follows,

as if he's grown weary of speech
and gone back to what was inside him
after the wreckage of words,

and the sound he makes is only
the sound of someone remembering—
a maze of fragile and translucent images

where he now is lost perhaps, gazing absently
at a pond in dappled light, listening
to leaves stirring in a wind on its way somewhere.

At the Hermitage

This morning, before light, the voices
of the monks at matins lifted the sun
into one more day of the Creation.

Now, the headlands lean
into haze, the sea milk-blue and motionless.
In silence the hours drowse.

Only a small dun-colored bird
rummages in the underbrush, hunting
for something I can't see.

I have been reading Po Chu-i. Unencumbered,
but for the years he carried, he chose the path
of solitude into mountains much like these.

The clear sound of a bell from the mist,
a heron lifting from a pool of water—solace enough
for him and, sometimes, for me as well,

but when I turn away from my book
the old disquiet shakes and frets at my sleeve,
and I can find no peace.

Sit in your cell, St. Benedict said,
and your cell will teach you.
The hours drowse, the dun-colored bird

with his fierce appetite for the present
is hard at work, the gentle Po Chu-i is gone,
and under words, under everything is silence.

O Lord of Silence, I can no longer tell apart
what was abandoned, what gained or lost—
so much, so many lives tangled into years,

and how would I not carry them with me
even to the border of your Kingdom
and beyond it, if I could?

Doppler Scan: Deep Vein Thrombosis

This morning a man passed his silver wand
along the length of my leg and conjured images
from it that shone on a screen only he could see.
But in the quietness of that room, I heard
sounds like a bass drum measuring a march,
and some like rivulets running among stones,
or a small beast scuttling through autumn leaves,
a wind shoving lightly reeds by a pond . . .

I don't know why I'm trying so hard
to find such pastoral improvisations on a theme
retrieved from the ghostly wreckage of a leg
that has endured so long and arduous a journey.
"Beauty is Truth, Truth Beauty," said Keats,
who was young and "half in love with death."
I'm neither, though what was beautiful to him
awakes each day anew among the ruins.

Cygnus, when old, looked up from a sacred grove,
and in a dazzle of white plumage flew
skyward into the fires of his name, singing
through the clear trumpet of his throat, a song
that one might choose to end on, when that arrives—
a swan song for the journey, like an echo
of beauty and love's deep sorrow, singing.

How It Is (Later)

"Something is singing in the grass,"
I wrote—oh, years ago—in a poem
that left unsaid what it was that sang.

The grass by now is parched, the white horse
in the poem has gone to green pastures,
yet something is singing still by my window.

Some words keep to shadows or slip off
in a bank of clouds, leaving
but traces of themselves; some, we chisel

into stone slabs to anchor our dead
among the generations, and yet the dead return
at evening with their tales and consolations

and whisper us to sleep like a lullaby.
We wake to the mourning dove's soft call,
the rooster's exultations to the sun,

each singing what was given it to sing,
timeless, separate from our dominion,
but of a world in which we share

a rising chorus of ambiguous songs,
even as we enter another day of our lives
in the loneliness of how it is.

Notes

"Haunted Heart": In Haden's 1991 recording of this ballad he superimposed the original 1947 recording by Jo Stafford and Paul Weston, fading his version into her voice.

"A Credo for Fallen Arches": My poem is indebted to Jubilate Agno, written by Christopher Smart (1722 - 1771),

"Nellie": The poem is a speculation based on little more than a long friendship. Nellie Fox is a Hall of Fame 2nd baseman. He played for the White Sox when they won the 1959 American League Pennant. To be truthful, Nellie might have been derived from the name of Thelonius Monk's wife; Monk wrote a well-known song "Crepuscular For Nellie," Phil was a jazzbuff, but then that would require a different poem.

"Big John and the Banjo": Sir John Davies (1569-1626) wrote a long poem, "Orchestra, or a Poem of Dancing," in 1595. His theme was the natural order and harmony of the world.

"The Garage": My maternal grandparents were immigrants from Piedmont, a region in Northwest Italy. Most of my family lived there, at one time or another; some were born there. The word brich, in our dialect, means "hill"; in our small town in Pennsylvania it was an area in which many Italians of the same region and dialect lived. "Grappa" was essentially Italian moonshine made from pomace. It is sold now in high-priced boutiques, and the Italians are still laughing in the counting house.

Supplement: Prose Selections, Comments, and Interviews

Introduction

The editors of this volume share Peter Everwine's opinion that the art speaks for itself and should be paramount. Even the artist does not know the full meaning of the creation. There has to be a reader, a spectator, a viewer for the act to have full resonance. We leave that resonance to each of you who read the poems. That is why we call this part of the book a "supplement" for in it we try to present Pete's words themselves about what he was trying to do and how, matters of secondary importance to the poems themselves. Three of the men who joined me in producing this book are poets with an enduring debt to Pete as a mentor and friend. There is a deep tie that binds practitioners of the same art—almost a blood family bond. You can hear it expressed by C.G. Hanzlicek in the foreword, David St. John in the afterword, and Christopher Buckley in the long interviews that follow. I am not a poet, nor was I a student of Pete's. From the beginning, Pete seemed like the brother I had been seeking; someone who understood me and whom I understood in a deep way that even blood brothers seldom realize and who shared with me some essential understanding of our lives in this world. We hiked together for many years with Bob Mezey, like brothers, into the canyon cut by the middle fork of the San Joaquin River. But every day each of us fished alone, meeting the wilderness on our own terms.

All of us were close friends of Pete, whose poetry and living presence gave us joy, comfort, and the belief that being alive and aware was valuable at every moment. We shared this feeling about Pete with many others, each of us in a singular way that met our needs. However, when we speak about Pete, everyone talks first about Pete's laughter. His was not like any other laugh; his laughter expressed something infinitely complex and infinitely simple about him as did his poetry. In one of his great poems, "Rain," he speaks of lying in a tent with his father on a rainy night and hearing

. . . .

a loon's wail
drifting across that remote lake—
a loneliness like no other,
though what I heard as inconsolable
may have been only the sound of something
untamed and nameless
singing itself to the wilderness around it
...

For all of us who heard Pete's laugh, we felt as he felt hearing that loon.

Bill Broder

II

The first selection in the supplement, published by *Poetry East*, was taken from Pete's computer along with the final poem that resulted from the experience noted. The essay illustrates how radically he distilled his passionate recollections over fifty years into the crystalline economy of a radically revised poem.

Concerning "In the Last Days"

In the late 1950s I wrote a poem about the death of my father; I called it "The Glass Tent" and the title alluded to a hospital oxygen tent transformed by metaphor into a deep sea diving bell. Separated from him by that transparent wall, I had watched as he drifted in and out of his final delirium. In the process of writing, I tried to use images that suggested what he might have seen—an old aunt, a tintype parlor, etc.— particulars of possible memories, all of them undergoing sea-changes in the metaphor of descent. The poem ended, as one might expect, when the glass cracked and the sea rushed in.

I thought I had made a marvelous poem, one in which I had found a language and a line free from the formal constraints I had been using. It was only much later that I realized how flawed it was. I had managed to load it down with fanciful images and turn it into a cartoon. I have never reprinted it.

I write of this early poem because "In the Last Days," almost fifty years later, grew out of its failure and a unremitting memory. And so I began again with separateness and the act of watching, remembering one of my father's gestures at the time, which became central to the poem. This time I wanted to stay close to the event, to speak of it directly and without unnecessary detail (stanzas one and two). More important, I now saw my father's death in a different and far larger world of time and memory, one that included my own aging and sense of uncertainty (stanza three). The shifting ambiguities of time and the acts of "seeing" or watching were charged with something more elusive and mysterious, and I felt a kinship with my father that I had not known in that early poem. Back then, I had been preoccupied with the process—and, yes, the delight—of image making. But I've come to believe that simple words and details grow powerful and haunting as they move back into the shadows. Moreover, a structure that is mechanical and one-dimensional is not equal to a form rising from resonant, complex rhythms of recurrence and surprise. Clarity doesn't have to mean shallowness, image isn't the whole of poetry, and form isn't a sack stuffed with particulars.

In the Last Days

In the last days of my father's illness
he lived on, separate from us in a tiny room
with a window in it, where we could look in and watch
him laboring at his heavy sleep.

And only once did he startle up
from the pillow, wide eyed, and slapped one palm
across the other—*Phsst!* he said, and smiled, and shook his head
as if in disbelief down into sleep again.

I don't know what my father saw then, wandering
In some mazy episode of time.
That was forty years ago. Forty years like yesterday.
Almost his own age now, I can see
his face before me: his wry smile of wonder
as if something had leapt up underfoot
in the dark and sped away
as he watched.

III

Feeling Back To That Voice—An Interview with Peter Everwine, 1983
by Jon Veinberg & Christopher Buckley

This interview was conducted in Fresno, CA, before Peter left to spend
a sabbatical year (1982-'83) in Israel and Italy. My memory now says it
was done in 1979 when I was living in Fresno and teaching at Fresno
State. Peter did not find the interview interesting enough when it
was done (Jon and I, about 30 years-old, no doubt doing too much
cheerleading) and it sat in a folder for two or three years until I re-
edited it. Peter approved of the newer tighter version and *Snake Nation
Review* published it in 1983. CB

Q. Do you remember anything from childhood or your early years that
may have had some effect on your work?

A. One of the things I suppose that happened was that my first language
was Italian, not English. I was raised with my grandmother who spoke
only Italian then, so until I was six or seven and going to school, there
were still occasions where I had difficulty remembering the English word
and I would substitute the Italian word, especially if I got excited, so even
as a kid I didn't come to know English at first . . . and I have a feeling
that's an influence. I don't quite know how, but I feel it has to do with the
sound of language, the rhythm of language, and I can remember that.

Q. Do you have any sense of why you started writing?

A. I came out of the army and I guess just about the time I was coming
out I was interested in writing—not poetry so much, fiction. And at
the end of my army business I wrote some poems and sent them to
Cid Corman, who at the time was editing *Origin* magazine, and they
were really awful poems, but as it happens you write an editor you've
never heard of and Corman at that time was publishing Creely and
Snyder, Levertov, the whole Williams factor that came out of the Black

Mountains, and so I sent him some poems and they were very rhetorical and odd poems, very amateurish. And he was extraordinarily kind. I've never met him. I've never had any correspondence with him except those first letters when I was young. And he was an extraordinarily kind man. He kept telling me that these were awful poems and who to read and to send more stuff and I would send more stuff and he'd tell me these were awful poems, read this . . . . And he had an amazing capacity, just energy of responding to bad poetry, and that was exactly what I needed at that point; I was in the army, I was isolated, I didn't know what in the hell was going on. And he was extraordinarily helpful, not because he published me, not because he told me what in the hell was going on, but because he was extraordinarily kind. And that was my first real contact with "a poet"—and so I'm remarkably fond of him in a very oblique way, because we've never met.

Q. When do you think you realized the concept of poetry that you now have? When did you start mining that background of yours?

A. Sort of late . . . I think after I got to Iowa, which is really where I began to take poetry seriously. Yeah, if I guess I had to isolate an influence that grew in Iowa, it would be Yvor Winters, in an odd way. And I don't think that the early stuff was sort of in the Wintersian direction. It was very rhetorical, very, almost archaic in diction, and I guess I didn't get back to what you're talking about until I picked up writing again which must have been about 1969 or '70 in Mexico.

Q. When did you stop writing? You went through Iowa and wrote there?

A. I wrote in Iowa, went to Stanford on a fellowship with Winters, and gave up poetry . . . about 1960, and didn't write again until about 1970, so there was a period of about 10 years when I didn't really write at all.

Q. Why do you think you stopped?

A. I don't know. I think I looked at the poems and I really didn't like what I was doing very much.

Q. Do you feel part of it was the influence of the poetry around you, the notion then that all good writing sounded a certain way, a similar way?

A. I don't think it was that theoretical; I don't think it was sort of an intellectual decision, deciding what's being written and what's not being written. I think I just looked at what I was writing and didn't think I was a poet—simple as that. You look at it and say, "that doesn't really seem very interesting or very good compared to what everyone else is doing," and so I think I just decided at that point that I really wasn't much of a writer.

Q. Well then, what got you started writing again? It wasn't really so many shots of tequila and the portrait of Poncho Villa, was it?

A. No, but it's as good a reason as any. I went to Mexico for a year; I didn't know what to do with that year. I had gone through sort of traumatic experiences, just personal experiences, and through, I guess, those experiences, it struck me that what I'd better do was to put my life in some kind of order, do something with it, so I was just sitting in Mexico in a kind of isolation, having gone through that stuff, just that need to start putting something down on paper, which I guess was an old need that I had just pushed aside.

Q. Did you discover the Nahuatl poems there?

A. Yes. That helped me too. I got hold of some books, and was struck by how extraordinarily simple and beautiful and clear and resonant those poems were and I guess I started to work with those and feed back and forth my own work into that. They were influential, I think, somehow they fit, if not my style or my voice or whatever it is one talks about in poetry, they filled some sense of need you have to be in touch with what you think of as legitimate poetry, and that was an important source I think; it fed something, if not by direct imitation, it feeds your sense of what is important in language, what is important to do with words.

Q. In the beginning of *Collecting the Animals* you mention that the Nahuatl word for poet means, "one who knows something." In "putting your life back together" and beginning to write again, was that done in order to "know something," to discover something?

A. I felt too that I was a, well it must be a common enough experience, that when things start falling apart very badly, you sort of weather yourself through that; you always feel as though you've sort of shed some skins—as if you're somehow, well totally new, you don't feel "reborn," but like with a different perspective for material, and I think I felt that sense in Mexico and that's what pushed me to writing again. And at that time I didn't think about whether it was good, bad, indifferent, career, or anything of this sort. It was just something that seemed to work out and it was good . . .

Q. When you were at Iowa, in addition to Winters, were there any other influences or models? Was Justice a help? Did others say, read this or that?

A. Yes, there were. Justice was there, Snodgrass was there, later on Phil, Mezey . . . I met a guy by the name of Don Peterson who was sort of the Dr. Johnson of Iowa City; he would feed me poems over and over again—not just contemporary poems but a whole range of stuff and that was enormously helpful and enriching—just people who were there constantly pointing out poems, talking about poems. It's easy to sort of downplay Iowa; now everybody who's been to Iowa says, "Oh yeah, that awful place" . . . and there were a lot of things that were awful, cliques, politics, but I bless that place. I learned more about poetry than I ever learned . . . it was tremendously influential.

Q. There's hardly anyone in poetry now who is not aware of all the poets who have come from or through Fresno and benefited enormously from the "Fresno experience." How do you feel about the teaching and all the people who have come through here?

A. The notion of having people come through who have been as talented as they've been . . . most of the time when you teach standard writing courses, students go out somewhere, they have a degree and they do something. People who have come through here and who have gone on to become exceptional poets—I don't know that you can take too much pride in that, in the sense of saying, "Jesus, I did that." It doesn't work that way. But to have that contact, that talent, seems to me a rich experience.

There are three of us here . . . I think probably Phil, I don't know exactly how Phil teaches, it's been a long time since I sat in on any of his classes, or how Chuck teaches . . . but I have a feeling that there are differences, because we do have differences in taste, different ideas about how we work, what constitutes a good poem, a bad poem, and this and so on, and I have a feeling that that exposure is probably good too—a sense of multiple things happening instead of one single voice or teacher.

Q. What are some of the models you're using now with writing students?

A. Many of the models that I start with are not even, I suppose, in that range called "literary poetry" . . . sometimes I do folk poems, tribal poems, sometimes oriental poems, sometimes I have different traditions—oriental poems especially, poems that just seem to be looking at something clearly, to get that sense of how language can deal with something very simple, very direct. So you start feeding models that way, hoping that they will catch something that's . . . it's not even literature anymore, it's a, maybe what you're teaching at that point is really the mechanization of imagination, so you're not calling it a particular kind of poem you're saying, look in all of these situations, how similar at times the imaginative process works. You can read an 8th century Chinese poet and he sounds a little bit like an African poet in the 12th century and he sounds a little bit like this poet over here writing in Greek, and what kind of pulls it all together? You say it's somehow similar to what people do with the imagination when it fits in terms of language, image, music, etc. . . .

Q. Perhaps then we're asking about ways of knowing, of finding things anchored in an identifiable human emotion. What about a poem we both like very much, "How It Is," would you say it is about as close to a poetic statement as there is as far as your writing is concerned?

A. That's a pretty fair statement I think.

How It Is

This is how it is—

One turns away
and walks out into the evening.
There is a white horse on the prairie, or a river
That slips away among dark rocks

One speaks, or is about to speak,
not that it matters.
What matters is this—

It is evening.
I have been away a long time.
Something is singing in the grass.

Q. This poem, by way of symbol, at one in the same time grabs what is most universal in the past and ties it emotionally together to what is most immediate in the present. Can you talk about the sources of that poem?

A. A little bit. . . . One of the responses to the poem that I like best, not necessarily my own poem, is that I like the poem that stays very close to the impulse, and I find that there is at least in me a peculiar sense of impulse to a poem. I'm aware of those poems that come from an occasion and you have to give information about the occasion but there's a way in which when you write that kind of poem you spend part of the time writing the occasion—I did this, I was doing that, this happened and it all leads to this. . . . And, I guess I get more and more interested in the kind of poem that doesn't need all the information coming into it, is very close to that sense of—it's almost a physical sense, a kind of suspended sense where everything is just about ready to break into meaning. I'm not sure where all those images come from, but it's part of that almost standing in the doorway of something, trying to catch that sense of the past, and a present, and a kind of presence, and I guess I want language to begin to intimate that sense of presence and stay a little mysterious.

I mean there are people you know—my sense of poets who have done this kind of thing—I think of the poems of Ungaretti which I love dearly, some of the smaller poems of Jimenez, even Machado. . . . And, especially Bobrowski; he has that sense of, it's a lyrical voice, but in touch always with that kind of imminence, and he's the poet among all those others I've mentioned who I really feel most is the spirit of poetry, or what is the spirit of poetry for me. I'm not trying now to talk about direct imitation of a technique or a voice, just that sense of where does the poem sit, for your spirit.

Q. Can you say something about the politics and the position and the ambition that you've sort of stayed away from?

A. My basic assumption really is that if you get too tangled up in the career of being a poet, you may not be a worse poet, but your character suffers. It's like any field where you get wrapped up in too much careerism; you may be very good at it but your character suffers after all. That doesn't say that to not get wrapped up in it makes you a sterling character, but the predictability is that your character suffers—it's an ignoble ambition to want to be a poet. Auden says somewhere in his notebooks, I forget the exact quote, talking about the character of the great poet, and he sort of makes the observation, (it must really be a cliché), that most really great poets, as characters, are assholes. There may be a real germ of truth as far as I can tell. I read the biography of Neruda and I much prefer the poems of Neruda to the biography.

Q. In the reviews of your work and in other places, do you think that the notion of Solitude and Silence is made too much of? We find more of a meditative progression of symbols and images, precise concentrations and not personal complaints—the poems take on the larger stance, the spiritual stance. Aren't you tired of hearing "Everwine and his silence, Everwine and his solitude," as if the poems were wholly about that—as if the white space on the page were really that important? Isn't it rather what you say?

A. I think I'm enormously aware of those qualities that surround the poem and I think that's more a matter of aesthetic choice, a matter of temperament. You sit down and you want to write a poem and there are a lot of other people who have talked about this, you hear a voice that you think is your own, and if you hear a voice other than that, it's not your poem; it's somebody else's poem which you can admire, but it doesn't sound like where your poems come from. And I suppose that sense of sitting down and listening to a voice probably comes close to a sense of a kind of meditative voice—that is what I begin to associate with my poems, that sounds to me the most authentic I can get. And I guess it also proceeds from that assumption I talked of earlier that I am less and less interested in writing the poem that is deeply occasional or anecdotal, or informational, and I want to stay very close to that impulse that feeds the poem, and that impulse for me comes very close to a sense of silence which surrounds the act of the poem, rather than one that is the center of the poem.

When I respond most to a poem in a way that's what I'm responding to; it sounds right to me, and it comes out and it doesn't sound quite biographical, it doesn't quite sound personally historical; what I want it to sound like is a hell of a lot better than what I am, or a hell of a lot wiser than what I am, or more knowledgeable, maybe that's all it is. It's a pitch you hear in the back of your head, a pitch, a voice and it hits, it's not like a note or anything, and that's the voice when you try to write the poem. You feel your way back until you can hear that voice, and if you hear that voice, you say, "Ah ha, there it is, let it talk," it's going to know what to say—and I think that's always the process. Maybe that's meditation, maybe it isn't, but it's feeling back to that voice until you hear and say, let it talk because that's the voice. And if it falters or goes into some other kind of voice, the poem breaks apart, the poem changes; it's not your poem, it's somebody else's poem.

Q. What about the term "witnessing" as something poets do? Isn't the strategy of the witnessing poem different than other occasional poems? The Italian poems in *Keeping the Night* seem to be very clear and beautiful poems of witnessing in which it's not this or that happened, but rather the right incidents or particulars have a cumulative emotional effect which do not resolve, 1, 2, 3, but altogether show us the right things or resolve emotionally that way. How do they work and why are they important?

A. Well in a way some of those poems, like the one for example about my grandmother coming on the train and so on, in a sense that poem was almost directly given to me by my mother who said, "This is the way it happened . . ." So in a way, in writing that kind of poem, it's a family poem, it's not in a sense just a family poem; I try to deal with a whole range that was personal and at the same time dealt with immigrant families and Italians at home, I suppose what you try to do in that poem is to locate the incident or the image, or the symbol if you will, that most releases the quality of that life. I've written a couple of poems about my grandmother—she was a wonderful woman, and I thought if I could release one of the real qualities of her life without being too wordy about it, just holding it to its own being, then it would work. I would say something about her and I would say something about my relationship to her and so the idea was not to comment too much or to give too much about her life, but to choose the moment that in a way most revealed her life, and that story I thought was the most revealing of the woman. So in a way that kind of witnessing, I meant it to go in a couple of directions, I wanted it to be a personal witnessing, of my own roots, my own family, and at the same time I didn't want it to get locked into a sort of biographical, anecdotal, informational poem—I wanted that sequence to play off the whole of one part to the other part, the man something different than the woman, a man and woman in relationship to myself, the village in relationship to what I return to, what I try to find, etc. So I think witnessing there is a . . . usually when you think of the witnessing poet you think of it in a kind of political context, witnessing some sort of political degradation, corruption, witnessing values in the midst of corruption, and that tends to put a political cast on the poet. Those poems weren't political witnessing, but I think they're trying to witness what is valuable in lives, what holds it to be valuable, my grandmother in a sense was nobody, a small Italian woman, she had enormous value for me, because in a way whenever I go back to her or think of her I know exactly what virtues, what responses are there, and I think that's a way of witnessing too; say this is what is valuable, this is what was there, this is what creates my own sense of work, my own sense of love. It's not political at all, but it's a way of reaffirming some kind of real continuity, and a kind of life that really doesn't have much continuity—I don't have much continuity, my children don't have much continuity. In a way, she gave me continuity, and I wanted to reaffirm that I suppose.

Q. The poem that witnesses, then, is a lot larger than those poems in which the poet simply recounts events, personally, saying, I didn't get this or that out of the experience, as opposed to making a larger statement about values?

A. I suppose the other quality attached to that isn't political. In many ways I guess, many of those poems from the book, certainly that sequence in the Italian poems, are elegiac; if they're witnessing, they're witnessing in the sense of mourning what's past, to a degree. So maybe for me that act of witnessing is often that relationship, maybe it always has that melancholy cast, I don't know . . . and that may be my temperament too.

Q. Your first book is almost like a celebrating of the past, rejoicing of the past, and you're becoming a part of the past. The second book seems to be more brooding, to have a lot more anger in it, more of a mourning of the past, and, comparing the first book with the second, what is the general turn of attitude?

A. I think the first book, for example, is more scattered than the second—it's less cohesive to my taste. The second book was very cohesive, and I think perhaps to a number of reviewers, almost overly cohesive; that is to say narrowed in range—some complained that the voice seemed too similar, that the poems seemed narrowed down in range, so that I tend to discount that. I like the second book better than the first book; it's a darker book, I agree with that . . . and that may be a number of things, that may be a matter of aging which is not to be discounted, it may be a matter of shifting of time where I'm starting to write again, to settling into writing, being truer to the elements that move that book. It may have been because I spent a long time alone doing that book. One of the elements I liked in that second book was its consistency, its voice. I have to agree it's a darker book in a sense that it is both narrower and much less openly celebratory or joyous if you want to call it that. That seems to me one of the givens that you have to accept, that if a book is of that nature, that is what's happening in the life, in the thinking, and you sort of accept it in its framework, and so I'm willing to say I understand the criticism of the book because it has darkened and narrowed in its kind of concerns, and then I have to really step back and say, but that's what I wanted.

Q. Despite the difference between the two books, despite the more celebrating and brooding side of each we read them as equally mature and spiritually realized. Would you agree with that?

A. It would sound arrogant if I did . . . . when you talk about childhood, for example, even if you exclude it from the normal terms of spirituality, it seems to me you can go several directions—you can write about childhood in the sense of what I did when I was in my past: I was a kid, this happened, and I had this relationship with my father . . . and sometimes you can write the poem in which childhood is continuous, present, that is to say it is not something that you achieve simply through recollection or nostalgia, or put in the framework of the poem as being time past, but in the framework of the poem it can also be time immediately present, continuous. And, I think one of the senses I have sort of using the childhood detail, the childhood image, whatever it is, is that it is absolutely continuous, it's present, and that's close again to my sense of getting at the impulse of the poem; when you don't feel your childhood as something sort of past, you feel it as an absolute, immediate, locatable present; it's there, and the ability to move in and out, in and out, and to hold it all at the moment, seems to me the most interesting possibility . . . not to just talk about it as I did that, or I was that, I am this! It's happening now! The moments where I'm most pleased at times in the *Keeping the Night* poems, is when that can occur, when the whole thing is flooded by that sense of absolute immediacy, but tempered.

Q. What role do objects play in the life of your poems; your use of objects is comparatively spare. Do you see objects symbolically?

A. In a way, I have a limited range of objects. I'm not terribly . . . when you really talk about a poet who brings a lot of objects into a poem you're talking about a catalogist, I mean that's really the art of bringing objects to a poem. I guess for me objects in poems have almost very little literal life. I bring objects into poems maybe because they have a start in a literal life, but for me, objects always take on the resonance of metaphor, or symbol, or whatever, and that's a fairly limited range. I think in most ways the vocabulary I use, the objects I use, are probably very simple, very commonplace. I don't think they're eccentric or unique or even very inventive. They always manifest themselves to me in some sort of special meaning, and I think that when you stay with relatively simple objects, they tend to take on more meaning than elaborate and eccentric objects simply because they've been around so long, or maybe because they've been in so many frameworks of literature or meaning or proverbs or whatever you say . . . or maybe because they are so familiar with our lives and those seem to me the most luminous for poetry.

Q. How do you see yourself standing in the world as a poetic voice— that is, your poems and voice are unique and totally distinct from any other poet or group?

A. I don't think I ever measure that. I'm not sure I ever clearly distinguish my voice, other voices, other styles. I think that calls for almost stepping outside your own boundaries for examining where you are inside that boundary.

Q. How do you see man standing in the rush of existence, the spiritual and human structures of existence? Would it be correct to say your views are not so much concerned with the immediate manifestations of our society, that your views could even be called primordial, elemental? Does this present problems for you?

A. My notion is that human beings sort of sit at the center of an immense desire. They desire things; it's simple, like other people or women, but a kind of immense longing that goes on in the world. I don't think I'm normally religious, dogmatically religious, but that sense of a . . . maybe it's a matter of perspective, maybe I tend to take a stand that's way out somewhere. I mean people talk about the lack of, to use a reviewer's phrase, "author commitment," if that means what I think it means . . . I guess I always stand way back from things and look at it in maybe a larger scope— I'm not that socially minded; I'm not that interested in the structures that we usually call social. I don't think I write many social poems. It's a hard question for me to answer because you have to be awfully self-aware of where the voice comes from, what your philosophy about life is, and I'm not so sure I've ever been self-aware of that.

Q. To go back a bit to what you said about the more simple objects of the earth being used in poems—wouldn't you say that they are more reasonably cherished than more eccentric or private objects or events?

A. I like a certain weight in language, and a certain weight in poetry, and I think, God help me, that was one of the things that attracted me way back then to Yvor Winters. It's very simple these days, and even then, to make great sport of Winters, his pronouncements, his judgments, his this, his that. In many ways he was a very silly and crotchety man, but I think what I most responded to in Winters as a critic and even more as a poet, was the immense authoritative weight that he had to his poetry, which I thought was synonymous with poetry at the time.

Q. Like his poem "To The Holy Spirit."

A. Exactly. That great heady voice, that a . . . he was almost baffled by experience, baffled by death, baffled by all the boundaries one walked into. And yet, there was that deep, grave sensibility, and that heaviness, and orderliness of language, and I thought, that's what poetry really ought to be. And I think I maybe haven't lost that, and I've abandoned the notion of rhetorical poetry, formal poetry; I think I've abandoned a lot of what Winters had, ideas of what poetry should be, but I think that kind of gravity of voice is for me always something I've found in poetry that I've loved. And it needn't be archaic, and it needn't be high-falutin—just a heavy seriousness, and I must say I've never been able to write comic poems.

Q. Can you tell us a little about folklore, myth, fable, and your own work?

A. I love fable. Fables are as close as I can get to being able to write in a different voice. I just finished talking about this great voice . . . the fable allows you to, in many ways, really release from that. It also does a lot of things; for one thing it tells a very nice simple story and yet keeps to a serious point, a point that isn't just locatable in an odd historical moment. It allows you to have more a sense of play than I might have in a poem; it allows me to have a little more whimsy than I might have in a poem. It's just that it opens another kind of small door or window and says, "Hell, you can do that and still stay within the strictures of what you think an art form ought to do," and still at the same time be fun to do. In a way, fables are more fun to write—sometimes poetry is lovely to write, but it may not be fun—fables are fun.

Q. Can you say something about "The Fish / Lago Chapala" from *Keeping the Night*—how do you see the primary rituals of people, say not even so much rituals, just things they do to survive which carry over to us?

A. You're referring to that little myth at the last section that talks about the tear pots—that's sort of adapted from a real myth. It's adapted from really the function of those tear pots; there was a real function, I mean they did collect blood. I think its value there is the same value as art, what it is is sort of a nonverbal dramatic enactment of their whole life meaning, I mean the whole life cycle. It's a prayer, it's a benediction, it's an acknowledgment of their lives, an acknowledgment of what's outside their lives. It takes no verbal form but in a way, like a ritual, it seizes upon the dramatic components of what their life means—you give something to the water, the water gives something back to you. I think it was my temperament that saw that act as blood and somehow pain. I'm not sure they did at all, maybe they did, but they must have, they knew better than that. I worked on it for a long time. I had the first section as an incident—the burial—and the section about the fish, everything turning into fish, but I couldn't find the link between them. I knew there had to be a link, and I think it was the myth that gave me the link—that is what myth always does, myth is that thing that creates connections, and it seems to me that the poem is that thing which creates connections. The two functions are very close together; if you can bring the myth and make it the same as the poem, then you've fulfilled something, you've made the connection, the significance of the discrete elements of our life—a burial, fish drying on the landscape of the road; the myth holds it all together, the poem holds it all together—you bring it into the poem.

Q. You have a marvelous poem of curses. Is that close to the fable concept, but say, a bit on the lighter side?

A. That's an old format, that notion of . . . in Italy I came across this; it's an old tradition that each village has its form of sort of making fun of other villages, and at every sort of yearly celebration of the village, they used to enact this, that is, it was a sort of literal litany of insults, and that's a very old folkloric element. It's one of those things that you can take right into your own literary tradition and make it work, but once again it's something that's been part of a literary tradition—it's something that's been valuable, it's something that's been persistent; it's useable as any literary tradition of Keats or Shelly or anyone else and it's also marvelous fun. It's the old premise, one of the old definitions of the poem, or the old definition of language—you reach out and you name something, you name it and you got it. This is a way of naming, the folk tradition names, the poem names; if you name it you can identify what you love in the world, you can identify what you hate in the world, and to do that is to recognize it. Or to put it another way to come back to an earlier question, it's a kind of witnessing, you name it and say, "There it is," and that just to witness in a way—so that's the old tradition.

Q. About translations—you've just published a collection of poems by Natan Zach. What moved you to do him? What's special or unique about him, and then again, how do you choose who you translate, and what if any effect does translating have on your own work?

A. Well I think in the case of Zach, I got exposed to a few of his poems. Shula read me a few of his poems and I liked what I heard, and so I began doing some for the sake of doing some, without any sense that I would go much further than that. And then it seemed to me that I got interested in him and you get interested in people for the strangest coincidences—he's my age, what is an Israeli poet my age doing at this point? He also doesn't write very much like me—in part yes, in part no—he's different. I feel a closer affinity to say the Aztec stuff if I were talking about relationships of technique and so on, than I do to Zach, because Zach is in many ways a very intellectual poet, that is to say he really does know how to think inside a poem. And, I think very few, this will sound very prejudiced, but I think in general there are probably in American poetry very few who really think in poems—there is thought, there is logic, there is metaphor, but there's not really any intellectual structure, and Zach is often a man who works in intellectual structures and ironic structures, and I found that immensely attractive, partly because I didn't know how to do it, because to a degree it's almost foreign to my own sense of writing and I thought maybe I could learn something. Because he really does sort of move through, and you can see it in a poem, you can hear it, this is a man not looking at self drama, but outside at a kind of problem, and thinking about it in terms of not logic but the movement of the poem and that's immensely attractive to get into that kind of poem and work inside of it without ever claiming it as your own. You say, "I wonder if I can manage this by somehow approximating his voice," and obviously approximating my voice because that's obviously the only thing you can do with it, taking it into your own language anyway. It turns out that to be neither Zach nor quite myself, but an amalgamation maybe, closer to Zach obviously than to me I hope, if I'm accurate in my translation, but he's a very attractive poet and he's a great ironist; he's really an ironist of allusion, experience, he's a wonderful poet. He hadn't been done, no one had touched him in the sense that there are very few English translations, and those available, with one or two exceptions, are just not adequate, that is to say they don't really capture what he's doing in a poem; they're not accurate, and he's damn good.

Q. Do you see Zach as sitting in the same areas of the theater as you are when we're looking at the big poetry screen as far as witnessing and staying outside of the idiosyncratic kind of writing?

A. He can be very idiosyncratic insofar as he opens himself to the possibility of, well for example the use of the pun—because he is using Hebrew the possibilities of the pun are enormous, sometimes almost untranslatable. But to sit inside the ironic usage of language as well by way of the pun and so on, to me is a relatively unfamiliar technique. I don't really see myself as an employer of the pun; he does it fairly consistently, so in many ways he is remarkably foreign from what I know as my own voice, what I'm interested in as a poet. He also seems one of these relatively isolated, to the side of things, poets—maybe that's why I like him.

Q. How is your Hebrew?

A. Poor. Shula is indispensable; I couldn't even come close to him without her notes, without her gloss. In some sense, she is really the co-translator of this work; I couldn't even get through him because his use of language is very complicated and dependent on a whole network of playing-off these Biblical allusions, and unless you have that awareness of how a language can play off and create ironies off the Bible, you're lost in Zach; you can't follow him.

Q. Do you wear, so to speak, two hats? Do you translate and then give yourself time for your own poems? Are they totally different; does one affect the other?

A. I don't really see them so much as two hats, to me they're involved with poetry, which is one of the reasons I suppose I include translations in my own collections. I don't see a hell of a lot of difference in writing a book that has your work and including translations of some body else's poetry—in a way that's your work too, and I sort of like the idea that you create a book that is not just your work in terms of your own original poems. You sort of touch base with things that are around you and outside of you, and sort of feed the book; that's why I put the Nahuatl stuff in the first book and why I put the Zach in the second book. I was writing a sequence of stuff that had to do with Israel and it seemed to me that after a while you are a literary person—you don't make those neat distinctions between literature and experience, I mean literature and experience go together for me, one feeds the other, vice versa, etc., very little distinction. So, if you're writing a section about Israel which concerns somehow the experience of that, well, the literary experience is part of that experience too. So Zach, the translations, tend to feed and vice versa; it's part of the same, to me, cohesive world, and why compartmentalize it and say, "Here, this is my work, this is somebody else's work—this is A; this is B.

Q. Who are some of the European and foreign poets you read? Also what subjects outside of poetry interest you, what books and writers do you think are neglected or overlooked?

A. I think I read most of the European people I can get a hold of. That's that strange balance I guess since Williams, since Whitman there's that notion that there is a distinct American poetry, a distinct European poetry. You create the American poetry and you abandon the European poetry, and I don't know, but maybe it's just fashionable these days. It seems I read an enormous amount of European poetry in translation, sometimes by way of almost a kind of preference.

One of the things the Europeans have provided is subject matter, I mean it really comes back to an almost archaic term, the very fact that they've been exposed to most of the important currents of history, that they've been witness to an appalling kind of history. In an odd way, American poets have almost been luxuriating in a sense of what could poetry deal with? What is the subject matter? What could it do? How can it deal with the real stuff of our lives? And I think European poets in part have answered that out of hand "It can do this!" Which is an odd way to restore—I don't mean to denigrate American poetry at all—but that sense of what really is the importance of poetry, what it can do, what is its value, and I think the European poets have an enormous sense of what it can do—that it's not just poetry that deals with self-examination, self-therapy, or this or that; it really has a legitimate way of dealing with the major blocks of experience: war, death, poverty—all these things. And I think that's been enormously influential, if only a kind of oddly therapeutic way—by God, poetry does mean something after all—here are these guys to witness that sort of meaning, that sort of coming to grips with experience. And also, because they're not locked into certain kinds of techniques that have become almost synonymous with us, and that's tremendously valuable as a way of sort of restoring one's optimism in poetry, if only that. . . .

Q. What fears do you have about writing poetry, about inspiration? Do you ever feel you're losing it or repeating yourself, writing the same poem? What about the element of time, etc.?

A. I think it's difficult to pinpoint what feeds your poetry, for any given person what feeds it, what creates not just a need to do it or to write it, but what actually creates the substance of it, and I think because it is to a degree somewhat mysterious and you're not totally familiar with it always, you're afraid it's going to go away. I've always lived with that because I go through long periods of time when I don't write, when I don't feel like writing, when I don't feel like I've ever written before, and those days are always scary. It's as if what ever came to you unknown has also left unknown; you are no more aware of its coming than you are aware of its going, and so I think there's that immense feeling that at any given moment whatever gift you had has become a failure and that you end up almost literally speechless. And I think that's frightening not because it has anything to do with money or fame or anything else, but because it is one of the ways that you value yourself and if you value yourself in that way and you find the way you value yourself is to a degree mysterious, then it's frightening, because you don't know that you can summon it back and say, "Don't go away."

Q. What do you look for in your work now? Are you working toward a third collection?

A. It's a mishmash at the moment. I never quite know what directions I've been going in. I sort of sit down and say, I'm pretty close to a book. I think the last book surprised me because it was so consistent; I didn't realize how consistent it was until I sat down and said, "Okay, it's about time to put it together. So at the moment, I don't really know where I'm going; it's not that close to being finished, about half a book. . . . The Zach's has taken up a lot of time—a lot of stuff I've not been very happy with also, I've put it aside or thrown away or said, "These are not quite the directions I'm going in." In a way, the next book is still very ambiguous. I sort of know what I don't want to do but I'm not sure of what I want to do.

Q. What is it that you don't want to do?

A. Repeat the second book. Not that I need to come out with something wholly new, I think that's sort of foolish—that sort of constant seeking for something novel. But I don't want to write the same poem over and over again. And I guess I don't know what to do with some of the darknesses in that last book. I want it to either get a hell of a lot darker or change some aspect of whatever it is, and that's been the problem so far—knowing what to pursue in that, how to step off from that book.

Q. Although *Keeping the Night* is darker than *Collecting the Animals*, what you have to say overall comes to some larger spiritual resolution and so doesn't that maybe take some of the burden off worrying about whether one is darker or lighter?

A. Yeah, I don't worry about whether it's darker or lighter, frankly. I'm not really terribly interested in whether it is or not, as long as it seems to be authentic, then I don't care really what it says at that point.

Q. What hope do you have for your poetry and poetry in general?

A. Let me answer the second one first as it seems to be easiest. I don't think you have to have hope for poetry, I mean I think it's independent of anyone's hope for it. I think that it is so anchored to somebody's need, I'm not talking about audience, but just somebody's need, that you don't even have to hope for it, it's like a given—and if it's not poetry, it's something very close to it, and there's no way to hope for its being as if it's in some danger of survival; I don't think it is. For my own poetry, what the hell can you hope for? You want to write another good poem, and after that, maybe you want to write another good poem . . . and that's all you can say. You hope for the next thing to come, that it will be right, that it will be good.

IV

Some remarks by Peter Everwine about his craft gleaned from an interview by Chard deNiord, in Grafton, Vermont on July 18, 2010. Published by the Iowa Review, *48/2 Fall 2018. Edited by Bill Broder.*

I came to Aztec poetry at a fortunate time. I hadn't been writing, had no idea of what it meant to be a poet beyond a vague idea of general ambition. The poems—I read them in Spanish—let me work toward a language other than what Phil Levine once called "the language of Princes." At that time I had no real knowledge of the Aztecs or their poetry, but I liked what seemed to be their way of rooting themselves into a world of simple things like birds, flowers, precious stones.

They had a vertical way of thinking. So you have a bird, but the bird is at the same time a mythic bird. And then it's also the soul of a warrior or a king. And they could collapse all of this into one image. I found it beautiful because it wasn't primarily visual, unlike the particulars so often found in William Carlos Williams.

It seems to me that what you really get in Williams, and what, I think, is easy to miss sometimes, is the energy in the movement of his images.

So there was always a way in Williams where the poems were kinetic. It wasn't just a matter of seeing for him; it was a matter of hearing that American voice. That quick, nervous voice.

I also don't work from a very large vocabulary. I think I have a very simple vocabulary. Very spare. And I don't know if that's deliberate; it's just the words that I react to. And I think at the same time what lies behind a word, its associations, and its resonance, its shadow, has been important to me. That may be a religious sense of the world but if so it's also much of the Aztec poetry I know—often a very melancholy view of the world.

It's the way I hear poetry. I don't know what the experience of writing poetry is like for you, or for other people, but it seems to me that my aspect of trying to write is really about trying to listen.

[Silence] . . . In the poem, and the language that comes out of the silence. This may sound like nonsense, but silence helps me to slow down a poem, to adjust a phrase or line or inner movement to its emotional weight.

The Aztecs ask a lot of universal questions about what life amounts to, and I think there's enough simplicity in their work that you're not ever afraid of imitating them. There's no sense of individual virtuosity in the Aztec poets, partly because it's an oral folk process, partly because they understood the whole system of symbols that was behind every word. I've never been very crazy about highly ornamental poetry.

I suppose if you go back historically—I like reading Donne, but I prefer Ben Jonson. These two poets seem totally different to me and I think of someone like Zbigniew Herbert, that marvelous poem where he says there are poets who close their eyes and a garden of images come streaming down. I don't think I've ever been in that position. And the thing is, I'm not sure I ever want to be in that position. I get plainer and plainer and sometimes I worry about that but there's not that much I can do about it.

Because I think it tends to push me towards a more garrulous statement, diffused narratives, bumbling around in the furniture of narrative, and I don't know if I'm very good at that.

. . . there are poems I've written lately that do seem much more given over to the narrative. And what happens, or at least part of what I think happens, is when you start using particulars, in that way of narrating the poem, the particulars tend to stay there as things, and I like particulars that sort of suggest everything behind them. It's a way of understating rather than simply stating.

I must have been influenced by other poets. But they are really hard to name. Yvor Winters, of course, some of those poems are wonderful. J.V. Cunningham, early on. Certainly a number of European poets.

I certainly read all those poets, [Galway Kinnell, James Wright, Robert Bly, Phil Levine] sure. And you know there were people who said that I belonged to the deep image school, people who said I was a symbolist, people who said I imitated Mark Strand's surrealism—I mean after a while, if you listen to everybody, you don't know who the hell you are. You know I had all those marvelous classmates. I mean the people you mentioned many were classmates of mine at Iowa.

Phil Levine, Jane Cooper, Donald Justice, Robert Dana, Henri Coulette: had to [have influenced me]. And that whole generation out of Iowa was a very significant one.

[Although I was adopted by my mother's second husband] I've never felt [my Italian ethnic identity] was concealed. I certainly never concealed it. I love the background I came from. It was rather funny when I talked about my childhood during my visit with Ruth Stone the other day, telling her I came from uncles who started out in the mine and so forth. She assumed I had a tragic childhood because of the word "mine." But I think I had a very good childhood, despite the very hard times of the 30s.

[My Italian father] died in a car accident before I was born. For the first years of my life, my mother and I lived in my grandmother's house in Leechburg, PA, and my grandmother mostly took care of me because my mother worked. I'm not sure how it affected me. Sometimes you don't really know what in childhood gets to you. My grandmother didn't know English. All the family that came to the house, my uncles for example, spoke the dialect. So as long as my grandmother was around, that was the language. A very loud language. And the language I was born into at that point was an Italian dialect. So in some ways, I know, that had to affect the way I listen to the music I hear in words. I can remember being in situations later on with my stepfather where I couldn't think of the English word and I would use the Italian. That was part of my growing into that family.

Well, you know, if you bring up a poet like Keats, I mean how can you not love some of those odes? They're so beautiful, they're so breathtaking, they're so heart-wrenching, but when it comes right down to the truth of it, I prefer Coleridge's conversational poems. I would rather read Coleridge's "The Nightingale," frankly, than Keats's "Ode to a Nightingale." I'm sure people would say I'm foolish.

I don't know how to explain it exactly. Coleridge is more intimate with his experience. Less aesthetic but more rooted. He's more colloquial, and he puts himself into the narrative. In "The Nightingale" where he holds his child up to the moon and the nightingales are singing all around him, what an incredible intimate moment that creates between a father and son and the world. And Keats is off listening to this gorgeous music lulling him to death and it's beautiful, he's so young, but it's so far away and there's so much language being generated. Coleridge has that deep gravity of his experience in his poem. And I think the last passages of that poem have a music that is the equal of Keats. You hear it again in Wallace Stevens, at the close of "Sunday Morning." And Coleridge is just saying, you know...

I think my sense of speaking in the poem doesn't create a very large public space, and I try, even in public readings, to create that private intimate space. I think there are poets who work wonderfully in public spaces, Whitman you mentioned. I heard when I was young Dylan Thomas read, and he just practically knocked me from my chair. I had never heard a voice like that. Or language like that, and although he was speaking about rather private experiences, the voice and the language were extremely public, I thought. I try not to. I don't think my speaking voice in my poems is public. I can do nothing about that.

Chard deNoid's most recent book is *I Would Lie to You if I Could: with Ten American Poets*, University of Pittsburgh Press.

V

In the Moment:
An Interview with Peter Everwine
by Christopher Buckley and Jon Veinberg

from *New Letters*, Vol. 83 No. 1 2016

Peter Everwine is one of the most accomplished and valued poets and translators writing in the United States today. His long and estimable career includes the Lamont Poetry Prize, a senior Lecturer Fulbright award for the University of Haifa, Israel, fellowships from the National Endowment for the Arts and Guggenheim Foundation, and an American Academy of Arts and Letters Award in Literature. "There is something shining and pure—a radiant clarity," poet Edward Hirsch writes, "a luminous stillness at the heart of Peter Everwine's beautiful, mysterious, and necessary work."

Everwine's recent collections of poetry include *The Countries We Live In: Selected Poems Natan Zach 1955-1979* (Tavern Books, 2011), *Listening Long and Late* (University of Pittsburgh Press, 2013), and the limited edition poetry chapbook *A Small Clearing* (Aureole Press, 2016), which is discussed here, along with recent and new poems, their sources, the lyric crucible and his recent achievements.

*   *   *

NEW LETTERS: I'd like to begin with a poem on the Poetry Foundation's website, "Designs on a Point of View," originally published in *POETRY* magazine (1958), which resonates still with the singular quality of your voice and vision. It is from your first book, *The Broken Frieze*, and it's a mix of Petrarchan and Shakespearian strategies, right? Despite the formal mode—compulsory in those days—can you hear any threads connecting this poem's voice to the newest poems?

Designs On A Point of View

Thus, on a summer evening, how the light
Will never startle birds or quite define

That tree, that port in air, unleaved to night
And thickening to an atmosphere no line
Will measure. Yet the swallow at his trade
Revels upon this density—the lift
To the stunting wing, the thrust and accolade
Of air that vectors to the fruitful drift.

Design means supper to the birds, not flight,
Not simply the release, although that, too
Is part of it. And the tree that shapes the night
Will also aim the bird, give contour to
A local habitation where the eye
Is rooted, where the bird defines the sky.

PETER EVERWINE: Lord, this is more an archaeological site than a poem. This was among the first poems I published. You have to dig down through the layers of allusions, derivations, get past that pompous drumroll of "Thus" and maybe you'd find something—a kind of phrasing, a way of teasing out or playing off meaning from a couple of simple images, a voice that a reviewer of later work called "disembodied"? What I like in the poem is the word "supper," especially placed against so many of the other words in the poem. And maybe "vectors." For an early, formal sonnet, it has its moments, though overly infatuated with literature.

NL: I think "The Train Station of Milan" from *Listening Long and Late* (2013) is genius, the true and objective pathos of one moment—expanding to indict all our lives—that one hopeful gesture in a train station all that time ago. This is the second half of the poem:

.   .   .

The old man surely is dead now,

and I am of the age he was
when I first saw him—as I see
him now—that winter afternoon

in Milan, his hand extended, palm up,
his fingers opening and closing,
as if he were setting free something
he held, if only for a moment,
then beckoning it to come back.

How does the first impulse for the poem develop for you, and how does
the sensibility of a "moment" become a discipline in your poetry? How
does the implication follow, no matter how subtle, about the notion of
time, our common mortality?

EVERWINE: I was raised in an Italian family; gestures are language.
I remembered the scene in the station years later, and "saw" the scene
again, but slowed it down, found myself in the old man. So now the
gesture was not only an illustration of the arc of memory but also an
enactment of farewell, loss, and at the same time a yearning for the
moment to return and stay, to welcome back—an impossible gesture
to our passing moments. The poem depends on time and our common
mortality, although I was hardly thinking of abstractions at the time of
writing. The old man's gesture was also mine—so much slipping away,
so much reluctance and yearning for its return, by any means. The train
station was the perfect setting for departure and arrival; without it, the
poem would not have come to mind. The man's small gesture suggested
an entire history.

NL: One of the qualities of your poetry that I find astonishing is how
you have maintained a lyrical integrity and intactness of vision throughout
your career, a great deal of which relies on memory and loss. "Drinking
Cold Water," an early poem like the more recent "Rain," infuses memory
and loss through the detail of water. How fundamental has the theme
of memory been in transforming the thought and vision of your poetry
over 60 years of writing?

EVERWINE: It's always been important to me, though in earlier
poems it may have been more veiled. As I've aged, especially in more

recent work, memory has grown more central because so much of my life exists in remembering and because I believe I've dropped so many veils, become more intimate and transparent. In a curious way, growing old has taken away some of the luxuries of poetry but also has given me a certain freedom to speak more openly and plainly. I've never worried too much about being fashionable, at least in my later years, but it feels terrific not to give a damn except to write with integrity to the moment.

NL: Recently, in 2016, you published *A Small Clearing*. One of the most memorable poems in that collection is "We Were Running."

> We Were Running
> *in memory of Annie*

We were running up the slope of a hill,
that dog and I, an early winter rain
beginning to fall, wind-driven and sharp,
the clouds so black the edges of the hills
were etched and incandescent. That dog
and I were running, the two of us
apart and yet together, and even now,
in the solitude of a quiet hour—the days
and that dog long gone—I can follow
those far-blown traces of unexpected joy
and find my way back again: heart wild,
lungs filling with the breath of winter,
and that dog beside me running headlong
into the world without end.

Can you speak to that instant you capture here? It is near impossible, as we know, to write an effective, unsentimental poem on the subject of a pet. The dog is a coefficient for that distilled point of life that comes back in a much larger way. It is just amazing. How did the gathering of specifics establish the moment in the poem and then lead to the suggestion of the larger themes?

EVERWINE: The opening is fairly exact. I really did feel in touch with that dog, the wildness of the day, that incredible joy and intimacy I shared with that lovely dog. The poem tries to return to that experience, a tracing of images back through time. Also, a key for me was the sense of "apart and yet together," which leads into the last lines and their implications.

NL: To us, few contemporary poets give more music and elegance to grief with such startling, vivid imagery. In recent years, your poems have softened in tone but heightened in brevity and the weight of specific experience. "Elegy For the Poet Charles Moulton," from *Listening Long and Late,* and the recent "We Were Running" include joy, loss, humor, and mystery all bundled together by metaphysical string. Is this a conscious act on your part or has experience led you there?

EVERWINE: It's a hard question, because it suggests an either/or choice. I like when an ordinary word or small phrase suddenly expands into more than one meaning, even expresses contradictions. That always seems possible in the act of writing. There's always the experience pushing at you to get it right; at the same time there's the possibility, the expectation or alertness of the poet who is looking for the word or words that will tear themselves open to you. I think this happens in both poems that you mention. How many of us have listened to beautiful music and felt so much joy that we weep? I don't think that our emotional lives are easily simplified.

NL: To continue along this line, "At the Hermitage" mentions St. Benedict as advising you, "stay in your cell ... and your cell will teach you."

At the Hermitage

This morning, before light, the voices
of the monks at matins lifted the sun
into one more day of the Creation.

Now, the headlands lean
into haze, the sea milk-blue and motionless.
In silence the hours drowse.

Only a small dun-colored bird
rummages in the underbrush, hunting
for something I can't see.

I have been reading Po Chu-i. Unencumbered,
but for the years he carried, he chose the path
of solitude into mountains much like these.

The clear sound of a bell from the mist,
a heron lifting from a pool of water—solace enough
for him and, sometimes, for me as well,

but when I turn away from my book
the old disquiet tugs and frets at my sleeve,
and I can find no peace.

Sit in your cell, St. Benedict said,
and your cell will teach you.
The hours drowse, the dun-colored bird

with his fierce appetite for the present
is hard at work, the gentle Po Chu-i is gone,
and under words, under everything is silence.

O Lord of Silence, I can no longer tell apart
what was abandoned, what gained or lost—
so much, so many lives tangled into years,

and how would I not carry them with me
even to the border of your Kingdom
and beyond it, if I could?

What has your cell taught you? What regrets might you have in writing poetry? Or to take it a few steps beyond: Is it possible through the art of poetry to grow into your own poems?

EVERWINE: I'm not sure if the poem is much about writing or the regrets of pursuing poetry. Poetry has been a good life. Silence and solitude are the conditions of the hermitage, just as they often are those of writing. The bird lives in the immediate; to go back to the beginning of this interview, "design means supper to the bird." Perhaps to live in the present—the bell, the heron—is enough. What the cell teaches me isn't the peace found in solitude, isn't the detachment one requires. What I find is what lies beneath the Word: silence. I bring to it my life, my memories, my history, and I don't wish to give them up, or can't give them up without becoming something other than who I am.

NL: A new poem, "Lines Written for Elmo Castelnuovo" [first published elsewhere in this issue] includes personal and family recollections, as we see in *Keeping the Night,* the small particulars from childhood that become emblematic for longings and insights we come to, usually later in life. I don't think I know a more powerful elegy. This poem in particular seems to have started with recalling that pat on the head—would that be right? Who are you recalling from your childhood in Pennsylvania? The specifics remind me a little of the Spiritual Exercises of St. Ignatius of Loyola. Is that fair?

EVERWINE: Elmo was my uncle, and I've written about him in more oblique ways. I grew up with him and my mother in my grandmother's house, a truly essential part of my life. I had a difficult time writing this poem. I had the first section but wasn't sure how to go on. I thought then to move the poem forward in time, then to return to him in the classic sense of emerging from the underworld to a vanished world that existed within me. In a sense, the poem built somewhat, unconsciously, on the gesture of the man in the station of Milan. The emotional center of the poem was the pale crescent of his skin that appears in the first section.

NL: Now, more than ever, the poems pursuing love of silence and solitude are wiser and much more haunting. How have these two elements affected your work and understanding of the world of which you write, and have they centered on your growth and learning through time, age, and absences, including your self-imposed gaps of not writing?

EVERWINE: I think "At the Hermitage" is perhaps the only poem in which silence and solitude are the major subjects. I'm really not sure why I've earned this reputation. I do write rather spare poems, and I often speak from a position of solitude. Also I often invite the speechless absent into a poem. I live a rather private life, though I'm far from reclusive. As for those periods during which I've not written, they may be a curse or a blessing, but certainly not a moral choice. I've not thought of myself as a career poet; I'm not claiming this as a virtue.

NL: At the memorial last February on campus at California State University, Fresno, close to 20 of us testified to the generosity and importance of Philip Levine as mentor and friend—many had been students. Your talk was easily the most moving, and you read a new poem you wrote for Phil, an elegy, titled "Nellie" [published in this issue]. You were Phil's closest friend in poetry and in the world for something like 60 years, and I know he depended on you for help and feedback on his poems. While most all the speakers that day were appropriately thanking and praising Phil, your poem spoke to the man, to a brotherhood, to a personal tenderness and common humanity you shared. Can you say a little about that poem and that relationship of so many years?

EVERWINE: I could never figure out why Phil signed his letters—and sometimes his books to me—Nellie, the name of an odd cat; Phil wasn't a man to have pets. He wrote a fine poem about a fox, and he had that painting of a fox that he dearly loved. On a pure hunch, and it is a hunch, I put Nellie and Fox together, which made "Phil-sense" to me. We both enjoyed, in a friendly way, sticking it to each other. Phil's fox poem suggests a world of anti-fops. I wanted also to suggest one of anti-fads. And I wanted Phil's spirit to have the last laugh, one true to the friend I knew.

NL: It's no secret that you have been a much revered and endearing teacher. If you had yourself as a student in this day and age, what suggestions would you have for him?

EVERWINE: Being a student in my day was pretty simple. Now you've got a zillion conferences, summer camps, lectures, poetry cruises, discussions, forums, advice, how to use flowers as inspiration, how to emulate suffering by wearing your shoes on the wrong feet, etc. Give it up. Find some poems or poets who move you; take them to heart. Feel like it's an honor to be in their company. I had, as a student, a small anthology by Oscar Williams. It was like a door into the Muse's bedroom. You didn't even have to knock, just open it.

NL: I want to go back to voice, and a new poem "The Day" [published in this issue]. It has always seemed to us that the great achievement of our greatest poets is to speak directly, to make the artifice of the poem disappear. I think of Levine, Kunitz, William Stafford, and Gerald Stern, and also of Milosz, Szymborska, Herbert, Jaroslav Siefert, and, of course, Antonio Machado. To present the specifics that lead to the universal in lines that are direct, clear, and yet luminous and exact seems to be the great task, and the true achievement of your poems, especially the new ones. You manage to have an idea as common as "happiness" grounded in this poem and then have it resonate to suggest a complex understanding of that in time. Can you talk about the voice and strategies of this poem, and, forgive us, the vision?

EVERWINE: Wow! What answer could follow that question? Vision seems so large a word. I don't want to over-explain what the poem comes to. I wanted to speak of a particular day, as sparely as possible. A day of happiness, a day without regret. Then, as it often happens in my poems, to move the experience in time, roughly parallel, and return to it in the light of a different or larger view, one altered by what had been encountered in time. I don't know if I'm approaching anything one might call "vision." It might be nothing other than reaching a certain age and trying to write as truthfully as I can at this stage of my life. Everything lies open to question. I have no answers.

*   *   *

About the Interviewers

CHRISTOPHER BUCKLEY'S most recent book is *Cloud Memoir : Selected Longer Poems 1987-2017* (Stephen F. Austin State University Press 2018) *Star Journal: Selected Poems* (University of Pittsburgh Press, 2016). His 20th book of poetry, *Back Room at the Philosophers' Club* (Stephen F. Austin State University Press), was published in 2014.

JON VEINBERG'S most recent poetry collection is *The Speed Limit of Clouds* (C & R Press, 2008). He is the recipient of a National Endowment for the Arts grant in poetry and lives in Fresno, California.

VI

Peter Everwine
From a Kenyon Review Conversation/short interview with Claire
Oleson (August 2018) in *Kenyon Review*.

There's a song mentioned in your poem of which the words, singer, and sound are never quite revealed. What do you think or hope this occlusion does to your readers' understanding or perception of the song? Is it meant to have a sound somewhere in thought or does the silence of the page do something to signal your persona's incomplete memory of the melody?

The first poem in my first book (*Collecting the Animals*) was "How It Is," a short and rather elliptical lyric based on a couple of images. The poem contained more silence than speech, and its last line became the beginning line of "How It Is (Later)": *Something is singing in the grass*. After almost five decades, I wanted to return to that poem, thus the present tense. The first poem was youthful, a poem stunned by the wonder and mystery of a natural world beyond a need for speech or explanation, a poem of renewal. The "singing" never had a particular melody; it was more metaphor than something that reached the Billboard charts. Since then, that world has become not less of a mystery, but one subjected to time and experience. An aging face often begins to reveal character, even its beauty. Both poems, especially "How It Is (Later)," are concerned with how limited words are in pinning things down, and what an extended "ambiguous chorus of songs" we hear in a world we love—one that now includes so many memories—knowing it will vanish with our passing. In that sense, the celebration and joy has acquired for me also a sense of loss and sorrow, which seems more complex and truthful.

The beginning of your poem quotes another, said to have been written before, does this poem exist anywhere? Does it matter,

to you, whether or not this poem's quotation of another comes across as authentic or humorous, real or in existence only in the reality and authority of "How It Is (Later)" alone?

I couldn't expect a reader to know the earlier poem. I believe one enters a poem on its own terms and, in good faith, goes from there; the poem stands or fails on its own, as does the first line. Whether real or imagined it finally doesn't matter, although it is an actual line I wrote. The movement and development of the poem is what matters.

How has your writing or writing process changed since you started out?

It seems difficult and unimportant to me to stand back and view a career of writing poems, even if I don't have a large body of work. My apprentice poems were formal; later ones more image-based, loosened and associative. I think of Zbigniew Herbert's depiction of poets who have "gardens in their hair." I'm not much good at gardening, and I now have less hair. I like rather spare poetry and try to avoid the overly narrative. I hope I've grown more open as I age, more interested in clarity than in drama or complex poetics.

Which non-writing-related aspect of your life most influences your writing?

In a curious way, my best answer to your question concerns the experience of growing up among the woods and streams of Pennsylvania. I learned to hunt and fish, both of which forced me to acquire a keen eye and ear, a sense of direction, humility and wonder before the power of the mysterious, the value of silence, a deep reverence for life and death, and the discipline of patience, all of which have been enormously useful to me in writing poems.

What is either the best or the worst piece of writing advice you've received or given?

In 1954 I got serious about writing poetry. I was near my date of discharge from the army and had landed in Baltimore. I read *Origin*, edited by Cid

Corman, who published many of the Black Mountain poets. Foolishly, I sent Corman some of the first poems I was writing.

They were terrible, of course, and yet Corman sent me a letter telling me, in a polite way, how terrible they were, but suggesting I should read W. C. Williams, among other poets, telling me to compare what I'd sent him to specific poems other poets had written. It was not simply a rejection but an entire lesson in how one might go about writing a poem rather then writing "poetically." And so we corresponded a few times after that, and Corman's generosity and patience were simply astonishing. Needless to say, he never published anything I sent him and I soon left Baltimore for Iowa City, against his advice, yet I am forever indebted to that man. He became even more helpful, in absentia, years later. So I thank you, Cid.

HOW IT WAS: An Afterword

I first saw Peter Everwine in 1965 or 1966 when I was a junior at McClane high school in Fresno and was attending every folk music performance that I could find. One night, some lucky friends and I found The Sweets Mill Mountain Boys with Kenny Hall, Frank Hicks, Ron Hughey and, of course, Peter Everwine. In the more than fifty years since that time, I've thought of that first sighting with more awe than nostalgia, as I remember Pete said almost nothing that whole evening, instead smiling, laughing his rich, infectious laugh at something Kenny or Ron or Frank had said, playing effortlessly his style of old-timey three-fingered banjo, and between songs smoking his unfiltered Camels.

It wouldn't be until 1967 that I would actually meet Pete, when Larry Levis introduced me to him outside the old Fresno State English department building. During those next few years, I was able to watch as Pete moved back to poetry, his own poetry, finding also while translating Aztec poetry the exquisite lyric simplicity and luminous beauty that would become the hallmark of his poems. In Pete's poems, I am always struck by the way the natural world awakens beneath his human gaze, at how the silence of that world holds for him an urgent intensity; and I am also astonished by the many ways even Pete's most narrative poems are, in truth, actual songs.

From Peter Everwine, I learned that there is no greater grace that can be experienced than discovering a poetry of unsurpassed integrity, dignity, simplicity and transcendent joy. Those of us who knew him think how very fortunate we are; and to those who are just discovering Peter Everwine's poetry, I'd say how very fortunate you are as well. Now, as we did, you are able to bring his poems into your lives.

—David St. John

Peter Everwine — 1930 - 2018

Peter Everwine was born in Detroit in and grew up in western Pennsylvania. He attended Northwestern University and the University of Iowa. In 1962 he began teaching at Fresno State and retired from CSU Fresno in 1992. He is the author of eight collections of poetry including *Collecting the Animals* (Atheneum) which won the Lamont Poetry Prize, *Keeping the Night*, (Atheneum), and *From the Meadow: New & Selected Poems* (2004) from the Univ. of Pittsburgh Press. Everwine's recent collections of poetry are *The Countries We Live In: Selected Poems of Natan Zach 1955-1979* (Tavern Books, 2011), and *Listening Long and Late* (University of Pittsburgh Press, 2013), and the limited edition poetry chapbook *A Small Clearing* (Aureole Press, 2016).

At California State University Fresno, with Philip Levine, and later C.G. Hanzlicek, Everwine was responsible for one of the most renowned creative writing programs in America—often referred to as "the Fresno School," though in fact there was no "school" aspect to it, given the wide range of talents and voices among the poets. Many nationally recognized poets today owe their careers and writing lives in large part to their time in Fresno working with Everwine, Levine, and Hanzlicek. The poets Larry Levis, David St. John, Roberta Spear, Gary Soto, Dixie Salazar, Ernesto Trejo, Kathy Fagan, Greg Pape, Jon Veinberg, and Luis Omar Salinas are but a few whose skills and poetic sensibilities were influenced and shaped at Fresno State.

Along with his poetry workshops, Everwine taught Eastern European poetry, Aztec, Swedish, Chinese, and Israeli poetry. He published translations of the Nauhuatl/Aztec, in a volume, *In the House of Light*, with Stone Wall Press 1970, published *The Static Element: Selected Poems of Natan Zach*, the Israeli poet, with Atheneum, in 1983, and then more translations from the Aztecs in *Working the Song Fields*, with Eastern Washington University Press, 2009. These voices and strategies had a deep effect on the poetry Everwine began to write in the 1960s and afterwards.

Everwine's long and estimable career included the Lamont Poetry Prize, a senior Lecturer Fulbright award for the University of Haifa,

Israel, fellowships from the National Endowment for the Arts and Guggenheim Foundation, and an American Academy of Arts and Letters Award in Literature. His poems were published in *The Paris Review, POETRY, Western Review The New Yorker, Antaeus, Field, The Iowa Review, The Ohio Review, Crazyhorse, Kayak,* and *Kenyon Review* among many other prominent literary journals, and his work has been widely anthologized for over the last fifty years.

CPSIA information can be obtained
at www.ICGtesting.com
Printed in the USA
FSHW011501250319